Pirate Attack!

By Deborah Lock

DK DELHI
Editor Nandini Gupta
Art Editor Shruti Soharia Singh
DTP Designer Anita Yadav
Picture Researcher Aditya Katyal
Deputy Managing Editor Soma B. Chowdhury
Design Consultant Shefali Upadhyay

First published in Great Britain by
Dorling Kindersley Limited
80 Strand, London, WC2R 0RL

Copyright © 2014 Dorling Kindersley Limited
A Penguin Company
10 9 8 7 6 5 4 3 2 1
001—195869—January/2014

A CIP catalogue record for this book is available
from the British Library.

ISBN: 978-1-40934-728-6

Printed and bound in China by South China Printing Company.

The publisher would like to thank the following for
their kind permission to reproduce their photographs:
(Key: a-above; b-below/bottom; c-centre; f-far; l-left; r-right; t-top)
1 Dreamstime.com: Ayzek09 (c). **20-21 Dreamstime.com:** Sarah2 (Reproduced Eleven Times).
22 Dorling Kindersley: Musee de Saint Malo, France (ca). **28 Dorling Kindersley:** Musee de
Saint Malo, France (b). **29 Dorling Kindersley:** Musee de Saint Malo, France (c, cl).
45 Dorling Kindersley: Musee de Saint Malo, France (c)
Jacket images: All cover images © Dorling Kindersley

All other images © Dorling Kindersley

For further information see: www.dkimages.com

Discover more at
www.dk.com

Contents

Get Ready to Sail   4

Queen Anne's Revenge   6

Chapter 1 Day 1   8

Pirate Rules   14

Chapter 2 Day 2   16

Cook's Secret Recipe   20

Pirate Sea Shanty   24

Chapter 3 Day 10   26

Chapter 4 Day 20   34

Treasure Map   38

Pirate Lingo   42

Pirate Quiz   44

Glossary   45

Guide for Parents   46

Index   48

Get Ready to Sail

"Ahoy there!

I am Jim, the cabin boy.

My ship is

the *Queen Anne's Revenge.*

So, you want to be a pirate.

Are you brave?

Do you love gold?

Yes? Then welcome aboard."

I will show you around the ship.

Hi, I am Polly!

Queen Anne's Revenge

Pirate ship from 1717

sail

deck

Day 1

Date: 1st July, 1717

Place: Port Royal

Weather: sunny

"Heave ho!
We are loading up food
and weapons.
Can you pick up this last crate
of pistols?
Follow me up the gangplank."

"Here is Captain Blackbeard.
He is the meanest pirate ever.
He carries six pistols.
See that black smoke
all around his head?
He ties strings to his hair and
sets them alight."

Wanted Dead or Alive!

Edward Teach
Known as Blackbeard the Pirate

Reward: **50** gold coins

(Beware! He is very dangerous.)

"Lift the anchor!"
says Captain Blackbeard.
The anchor is lifted.
"Hoist the sails."
The sails are raised.
The wind blows the sails and
the ship sets off.
"There is no getting off," says Jim.
"You are one of us now.
You need to know the rules."

Hoist the sails!
Hoist the sails!

Pirate Rules

- Everyone must obey Captain Blackbeard.

- Everyone gets a share of any treasure.

- Everyone can vote.

- Keep pistols and cutlass clean and ready to use.

- Lights out at 8 o'clock at night.

- No fighting another pirate on board.

- No stealing.

PIRATES WHO
BREAK THE RULES
WILL BE PUNISHED!

Punishments include:

 lashes on bare back.
Ouch!

 left on an island alone.
Help!

 shot with a pistol.
Bang!

Day 2

Date: 2nd July, 1717

Place: at sea

Weather: cloudy

Look out!
Look out!

"It is dark and gloomy below the deck.

Don't worry about the rats.

They run about everywhere.

You will soon get used to them."

Do you know what the galley is? (see page 45)

Here is Cook.

"Have you come to help me
in the galley?" asks Cook.
"Do taste this chicken bone soup.
Some more salt might make it
taste better!
This is the last of the chickens.
We will be eating
hard tack biscuits until
we catch our next turtle."

Give us
a biscuit!

Cook's Secret Recipe for Hard Tack Biscuits

300 g (3 cups) flour
120 ml (1 cup) water
6 pinches of salt

Ask an adult to help.
Set oven at 200°C (400°F).

1. Mix the flour, water and salt.

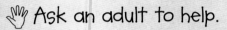

2. Press the dough onto a baking tray until thumb-nail thick.

3. Cook in a very hot oven for an hour.

4. Cut into finger—length squares.

Punch holes in rows with a fork.

5. Flip them over.
Put them back in the oven for at least half an hour until dried out.

They will be hard as tacks!

Black weevils love to eat them!

"We cannot stand around chatting in the galley," says Jim. "There is work to be done on the deck.

Sharpen the cutlasses.
Scrub the decks.

Shall we sing a sea shanty while
we work, my lads?
Strike up the drums and fiddles.
Can you sing along, too?"

Sing as loud as you can!

Pirate Sea Shanty

A pirate's life is the life for me.

Yo ho ho and a bottle of rum!

On a ship so fine we'll sail out to sea.

Yo ho ho and a bottle of rum!

Here with my hearties, we'll travel the waves,

And those who cross us end up in their graves.

We fight to the last.
We are brave and so bold,

And share out the treasure
of glittering gold.

So sing loud the tune and
bang on the drum.

Yo ho ho and a bottle of rum!

In the sea shanty,
what words rhyme
with rum and gold?

What was the treasure?

What is a heartie?

Day 10

Date: 10th July, 1717

Place: at sea

Weather: sunny

"Let us climb the rigging.
Check that the knots
on the ropes are tight.
We are very high.
We can see a long way
from here.
Sail, ho!
There is another ship."

"All hands on deck,"
cries Captain Blackbeard.
"Let us join the others," says Jim.
The pirates vote to follow and
then attack the ship.
"Make ready!"
shouts Captain Blackbeard.
"Get your weapons ready,"
says Jim.
"You will need:

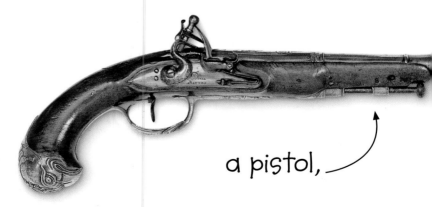

a pistol,

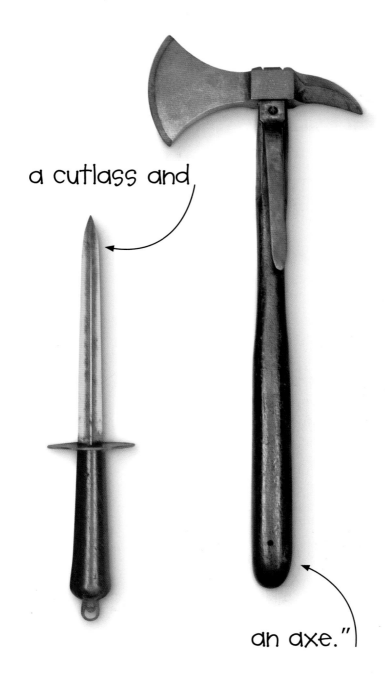

a cutlass and

an axe."

The ship sails closer and closer.
"Hoist the Jolly Roger!"
shouts Captain Blackbeard.
"The flag shows that
we are pirates," says Jim.

Bang!

"Do not jump.
That was the cannon shot
to warn the other ship's crew.
Will they give us their gold
without a fight?"

"They do not.

Get ready to attack!

Raise the red flag.

We fight to the death.

Throw hooks to pull
the ships together.
Swing across from the rigging.
Then fight with all you have got.
Hooray! We have won."

Day 20

Date: 20th July, 1717

Place: near Treasure Island

Weather: stormy

"What a great battle!

We take the gold.

Oh no!

The storm clouds are coming.

Those waves are huge."

Whoosh!

"Hold on!

Our ship will be smashed

if we hit a rock."

The sea is calm again.

"Land ahoy!" cries a pirate.

"There is our island," says Jim.

"We will sail around to the bay
so that we cannot be seen."

Splash!

The anchor is put down.

"I have the map of the island.
We have to find
the treasure chest."

Gold and silver!
Gold and silver!

Treasure Map

1. Begin at the 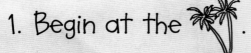.

2. Take 6 paces east to 💀 rock.

3. Beware of the 🦀.

4. Take 10 paces south to Black 🌲🌲🌲.

5. Use your ⚔ to cut the branches.

6. Take 3 paces north to ✖.

7. Use your ⛏ to dig 10 handle-lengths down.

8. Lower the 🪢 and pull up the 🧰.

Captain Blackbeard unlocks
the chest and lifts the lid.
The gems sparkle inside.
"We are rich!" shout the pirates.
Every pirate will have his share.
"Come and join the pirate party,"
says Jim.
"Yo ho ho!
It is a pirate's life for you
and me!"

Pirate Lingo

Pirates have their own way of speaking. Here are some words that you will need to know if you want to be a pirate too.

Yo ho ho!
(Say when happy)

Ahoy, me hearties!
(Hello, my friends)

Pieces of eight!
(Coins)

Seadog
(An old pirate)

Heave ho!
(Push)

Aaaarrrggghhh!
(Say when angry)

Shiver me timbers!
(Say when shocked)

Booty!
(Treasure)

Pirate Quiz

1. What did Captain Blackbeard have in his hair?

2. What was the name of the ship?

3. What was the name of the biscuits?

4. What was the Jolly Roger?

5. Who worked in the galley?

 Answers on page 48.

Glossary

anchor something heavy used to stop the ship from moving

deck floor of a ship

cutlass short sword with a curved blade

galley kitchen on a ship

gangplank ramp used to get onto a ship

sea shanty song sung by a sailor

treasure pile of gems and other objects that cost a lot

weapon tool used for fighting, such as a pistol

Guide for Parents

DK Reads is a three-level interactive reading adventure series for children, developing the habit of reading widely for both pleasure and information. These chapter books have an exciting main narrative interspersed with a range of reading genres to suit your child's reading ability, as required by the National Curriculum. Each book is designed to develop your child's reading skills, fluency, grammar awareness, and comprehension in order to build confidence and engagement when reading.

Ready for a *Beginning to Read* book

YOUR CHILD SHOULD

- be using phonics, including consonant blends, such as bl, gl and sm, to read unfamiliar words; and common word endings, such as plurals, ing, ed and ly.

- be using the storyline, illustrations and the grammar of a sentence to check and correct his/her own reading.

- be pausing briefly at commas, and for longer at full stops; and altering his/her expression to respond to question, exclamation and speech marks.

A VALUABLE AND SHARED READING EXPERIENCE

For many children, reading requires much effort but adult participation can make this both fun and easier. So here are a few tips on how to use this book with your child.

TIP 1 Check out the contents together before your child begins:

- read the text about the book on the back cover.

- read through and discuss the contents page together to heighten your child's interest and expectation.

- make use of unfamiliar or difficult words on the page in a brief discussion.

- chat about the non-fiction reading features used in the book, such as headings, captions, recipes, lists or charts.

TIP 2 Support your child as he/she reads the story pages:

- give the book to your child to read and turn the pages.
- where necessary, encourage your child to break a word into syllables, sound out each one and then flow the syllables together. Ask him/her to reread the sentence to check the meaning.
- when there's a question mark or an exclamation mark, encourage your child to vary his/her voice as he/she reads the sentence. Demonstrate how to do this if it is helpful.

TIP 3 Praise, share and chat:

- the factual pages tend to be more difficult than the story pages, and are designed to be shared with your child.
- ask questions about the text and the meaning of the words used. These help to develop comprehension skills and awareness of the language used.

A FEW ADDITIONAL TIPS

- Try and read together everyday. Little and often is best. These books are divided into manageable chapters for one reading session. However after 10 minutes, only keep going if your child wants to read on.
- Always encourage your child to have a go at reading difficult words by themselves. Praise any self-corrections, for example, "I like the way you sounded out that word and then changed the way you said it, to make sense."
- Read other books of different types to your child just for enjoyment and information.

Series consultant **Shirley Bickler** is a longtime advocate of carefully crafted, enthralling texts for young readers. Her LIFT initiative for infant teaching was the model for the National Literacy Strategy Literacy Hour, and she is co-author of *Book Bands for Guided Reading* published by Reading Recovery based at the Institute of Education.

Index

anchor 7, 13, 37

biscuits 19, 20–21

cabin boy 4

cannon 7, 31

Captain Blackbeard 10, 13, 14, 28, 30, 41

Cook 18, 19, 20

crew 7

flag 30, 32

gold 4, 10, 25, 31, 35

map 37, 38

parrot 7

pistol 9, 10, 14, 15, 28

rats 17

treasure 14, 25, 37

weapons 9, 28

Answers to the Pirate Quiz:
1. Smoking cords; 2. Queen Anne's Revenge;
3. Hard tack; 4. A flag; 5. Cook.